Exploring Che Reactions

A High School Chemistry Workbook with Answers

(300+ Practice Problems)

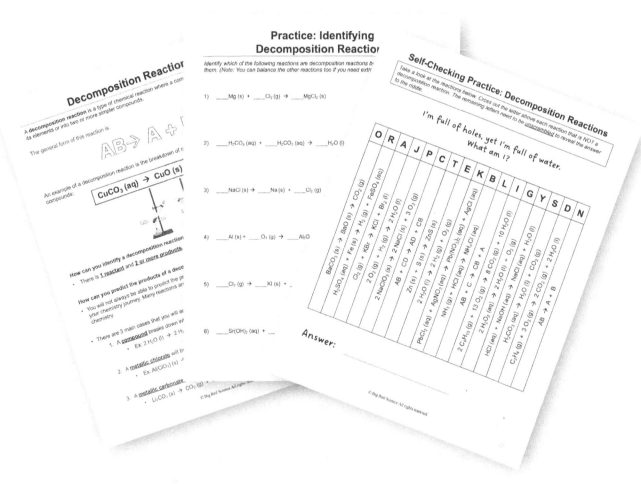

✓ **Classify Chemical Reactions**
✓ **Predict Products**
✓ **Balance Chemical Equations**

Table of Contents

Instructions for Use

Learning to classify, balance, and predict products of chemical reactions is a *crucial skill* for any chemistry student. It is also a skill that requires *a lot of practice* to master.

This content is designed to scaffold types of chemical reactions in a way that has students focus on one new reaction at a time and then practice working with it. From there, they will do *Mixed Practice* work pages that combine everything they have learned up until that point.

The workbook should be completed in the order it is presented, as each skill builds on what was learned before. The topics included in this workbook are:

- **Balancing Chemical Equations**
- **Synthesis Reactions**
- **Decomposition Reactions**
- **Single Displacement Reactions**
- **Double Displacement Reactions**
- **Neutralization Reactions**
- **Combustion Reactions**

For each topic, this workbook includes:

Short Lessons
Each new topic begins with a short lesson. It includes an explanation of the new topic and step-by-step instructions on how to identify the reactions and predict their products.

Practice: Identifying and Balancing
Each lesson is followed by a page of straightforward questions where students must identify the highlighted reaction type and balance them. Answers are found at the end of the workbook.

Practice: Predicting Products
After identifying the highlighted reaction type, students will have a series of 12 chemical reactions where only the reactants are shown. They must predict the products and balance their work. Answers are found at the end of the workbook.

Self-Checking Practice
Each section contains a self-checking practice worksheet, where students can practice their new skills to reveal a secret message or the answer to a riddle. They will know if they are right if these messages make sense! These self-checking practice worksheets are designed for students to be able to find and correct their own mistakes.

Mixed Practice
Each section is followed by *Mixed Practice*, which mixes each new reaction type into questions that may require identifying reaction types, predicting products, and balancing. These worksheets combine everything that has been learned up until that point.

Overview of Chemical Reactions

Chemical reactions, also known as **chemical changes**, occur when substances interact to form new substances. During a chemical reaction, the bonds between atoms are broken and rearranged, resulting in the formation of different substances with different properties.

When performing an experiment, signs that a chemical change has occurred include things like a color change, formation of gas (i.e. bubbles!), a temperature change, a new smell, or the formation of a *precipitate.

Chemical Equations

We can show that a chemical reaction has taken place by writing a **chemical equation**. Chemical equations can be written in a couple of ways:

1) Word Equation

A word equation describes a chemical reaction using words, for example:

> ### Iron + oxygen → iron (II) oxide

The substances to the *left* of the arrow are the starting materials, or the **reactants**.

The substances to the *right* of the arrow are the substances that are produced, or the **products**.

2) Chemical Equation

A chemical equation represents the same reaction using chemical formulas and symbols:

> ### $6\ Fe\ (s)\ +\ 2\ O_2\ (g)\ \rightarrow\ 3\ Fe_2O_3\ (s)$

In this example, "6 Fe" indicates six atoms of iron, "2 O_2" represents two molecules of oxygen, and "3 Fe_2O_3" shows three **formula units of iron (II) oxide.

We use (s), (l), (g), and (aq) to indicate the physical state of a reactant or product. These stand for *solid*, *liquid*, *gas*, and *aqueous solution*, respectively.

*a precipitate is a solid that forms when two solutions are mixed
**a formula unit is the proper term used when "counting" ionic compounds.

The Law of Conservation of Mass

The Law of Conservation of Mass is a fundamental principle in chemistry. It states that in any chemical reaction, **the total mass of the reactants is equal to the total mass of the products**.

Let's break down this law using the example of an aqueous solution of calcium chloride mixing with an aqueous solution of sodium sulfate.

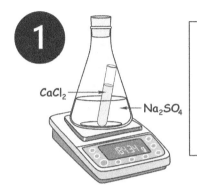

The set-up to the left shows a flask with a stopper in it. The reactants are **calcium chloride** and **sodium sulfate**.

Both are clear, *aqueous solutions*, meaning that the solid ionic compounds were dissolved in water.

They haven't mixed yet, and the total mass of the system is **184.34 g**.

The flask is picked up and turned over so that the calcium chloride is released from the test tube and mixes with the sodium sulfate.

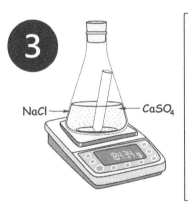

A chemical reaction happens when the solutions mix. The solution turns from clear to an opaque white color as a solid precipitate forms. This precipitate will eventually settle to the bottom of the flask.

Scientists have studied these types of reactions and know that the solid, white precipitate is **calcium sulfate**. The liquid portion in the flask is a **sodium chloride** solution.

Although we now have new substances, the total mass of the system is *still* **184.34 g**.

The mass of the system remains **exactly the same**, as matter cannot be created or destroyed – only *rearranged*!

The chemical equation that describes this chemical reaction is shown here:

$$CaCl_2 \text{ (aq)} + Na_2SO_4 \text{ (aq)} \rightarrow CaSO_4 \text{ (s)} + 2\ NaCl \text{ (aq)}$$

Balancing Chemical Equations

Now that we understand the **Law of Conservation of Mass**, we need to explore how to implement it in chemistry. It means that we have to know how to *balance chemical equations*.

Take a look at the chemical equation below:

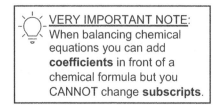 $$CaCl_2 \text{ (aq)} + Na_2SO_4 \text{ (aq)} \rightarrow CaSO_4 \text{ (s)} + NaCl \text{ (aq)}$$

This is the **skeleton equation** that describes the reaction on the previous page. Skeleton equations show the chemical formulae for the reactants and products, but they are not necessarily *balanced*.

If you count the number of atoms of an element on the reactants side, it needs to be equal to the number of atoms of the element on the products side.

# of atoms in reactants	Element	# of atoms in products
1	Ca	1
2	Na	1
1	SO_4	1
2	Cl	1

The skeleton equation above is *not balanced* because there are more Na and Cl atoms in the reactants than there are in the products. If we were to leave the equation like this, it would imply that some sodium and chlorine had disappeared during the reaction…this isn't possible!

Steps to Balancing Chemical Equations:

1. Write out the **skeleton equation**.

2. Count the **number of atoms** of each type of element on either side of the arrow. *If you have the same polyatomic ions on both sides, you can count them as one unit to save you time!* (Note: You may wish to set up a table for this like we did above. This helps when you're learning or when you have a particularly tricky reaction).

3. Follow the **MINOH acronym** and multiply the formulas by an appropriate coefficient until all the atoms are balanced.

4. Keep checking whether the numbers of each type of atom on both sides are **balanced**.

VERY IMPORTANT NOTE: When balancing chemical equations you can add **coefficients** in front of a chemical formula but you CANNOT change **subscripts**.

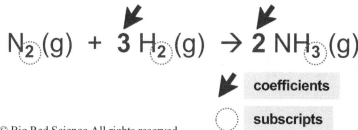

$$N_2 \text{ (g)} + 3\,H_2 \text{ (g)} \rightarrow 2\,NH_3 \text{ (g)}$$

coefficients

subscripts

Balancing Chemical Equations

Let's use the steps on p. 8 to balance the skeleton equation:

1. Write out the **skeleton equation**.

$$\_\_\_CaCl_2 \text{ (aq)} + \_\_\_Na_2SO_4 \text{ (aq)} \rightarrow \_\_\_CaSO_4 \text{ (s)} + \_\_\_NaCl \text{ (aq)}$$

2. Count the number of atoms of each type of element on either side of the arrow. *If you have the same polyatomic ions on both sides, you can count them as one unit to save you time!*

# of atoms in reactants	Element	# of atoms in products
1	Ca	1
2	Na	1
1	SO$_4$	1
2	Cl	1

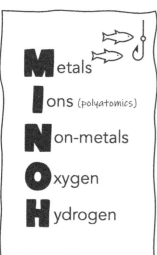

Metals
Ions (polyatomics)
Non-metals
Oxygen
Hydrogen

3. Follow the **MINOH acronym** to determine to determine the order you should balance things. Multiply the formulas by an appropriate coefficient until all the atoms are balanced.

4. As you add coefficients, **keep checking** whether the numbers of each type of atom on both sides are balanced.

MINOH says to balance metals first. We already have 1 Ca on each side, but our Na is not balanced. We will add a coefficient of 2 in front of NaCl to balance Na.

$$\_\_\_CaCl_2 \text{ (aq)} + \_\_\_Na_2SO_4 \text{ (aq)} \rightarrow \_\_\_CaSO_4 \text{ (s)} + \mathbf{2} \text{ NaCl (aq)}$$

Adding that coefficient also changed the number of Cl. Let's update the table.

# of atoms in reactants	Element	# of atoms in products
1	Ca	1
2	Na	~~1~~ 2
1	SO$_4$	1
2	Cl	~~1~~ 2

All elements are balanced now! We're done!

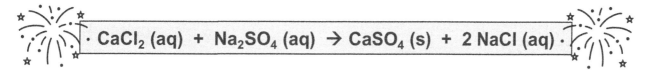

$$CaCl_2 \text{ (aq)} + Na_2SO_4 \text{ (aq)} \rightarrow CaSO_4 \text{ (s)} + 2 \text{ NaCl (aq)}$$

Self-Checking Practice: Balanced or Unbalanced?

Study each reaction and determine if it is balanced. Highlight the correct answer and place the corresponding letters in the blank spaces at the bottom of the page from 1 to 13. A message will appear!

#	Reaction	Balanced	Not Balanced
7	6 CH_4 (g) + O_2 → CO_2 (g) + 2 H2O (g)	**OFCO**	**ANDN**
1	2 Na (s) + $CaSO_4$ (aq) → Ca (s) + Na_2SO_4 (aq)	**LO**	**DI**
5	2 H_2O_2 (aq) → 2 H_2O (l) + 3 O_2 (g)	**PLU**	**STA**
10	HCl (aq) + 2 NaOH (aq) → 2 NaCl (aq) + H_2O (l)	**CAT**	**TYO**
13	2 H_2 (g) + O_2 (g) → 2 H_2O (l)	**ET**	**TO**
3	5 Fe (s) + 3 O_2 (g) → 2 Fe_2O_3 (s)	**MOCI**	**PATT**
11	N_2 (g) + H_2 (g) → 3 NH_3 (g)	**FL**	**UR**
4	Mg (s) + 2 HCl (aq) → $MgCl_2$ (aq) + 2 H_2 (g)	**RA**	**HE**
9	Mg (s) + O_2 (g) → 2 MgO (s)	**MIT**	**WNA**
12	2 C_2H_2 (g) + 5 O_2 (g) → 4 CO_2 (g) + 2 H_2O (l)	**FE**	**LA**
8	SO_3 (g) + H_2O (l) → H_2SO_4 (aq)	**OTDO**	**EINS**
2	2 Li (s) + F_2 (g) → 2 LiF (s)	**OKU**	**LOU**
6	HNO_3 (aq) + KOH (aq) → KNO_3 (aq) + H_2O (l)	**RS**	**TS**

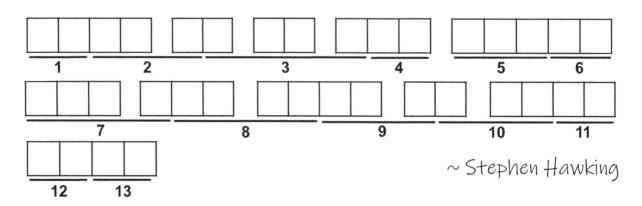

~ Stephen Hawking

Synthesis Reactions

A **synthesis reaction** (also known as a combination reaction) is a type of chemical reaction where two or more substances combine to form a single, more complex product.

The general form of this reaction is:

An example of a synthesis reaction is the formation of sodium chloride from its elements:

$$Cl_2 \text{ (g)} + Na \text{ (s)} \rightarrow NaCl \text{ (s)}$$

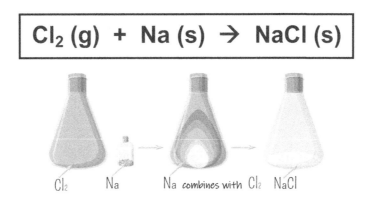

Cl_2 Na   Na combines with Cl_2 NaCl

How can you identify a synthesis reaction?

*   There are **2 or more reactants** and only **1 product**.

How can you predict the products of a synthesis reaction?

*   You will not *always* be able to predict the products of a synthesis reaction at this stage of your chemistry journey. Many reactions are complex and beyond the scope of high school chemistry.

*   There are 3 main cases that we can recognize and predict products:

    1. A **metal** and a **nonmetal** react to form a binary *ionic compound*.

        *   *Ex:* Cl_2 (g) + Na (s) → NaCl (s)

            Product is a solid

            > Use your knowledge of ionic charges (and the Zero-Sum rule or Criss-Cross method) to determine how many of each element will form the compound.

    2. A **non-metallic oxide** reacts with **water** to form an *acid*.

        * SO_3 (g) + H_2O (l) → H_2SO_4 (aq)

            Product is aqueous

    3. A **metallic oxide** reacts with **water** to form a *base*.

        *   CaO (s) + H_2O (l) → $Ca(OH)_2$ (aq)

            Product is aqueous

11

Practice: Identifying Synthesis Reactions

Identify which of the following reactions are synthesis reactions by circling **synthesis**. *Balance them. (Note: You can balance the other reactions too if you need extra practice!)*

1) ____Na (s) + ____Cl_2 (g) → ____NaCl (s)

synthesis   not synthesis

2) ____NaOH (aq) + ____H_2SO_4 (aq) → ____Na_2SO_4 (aq) + ____H_2O (l)

synthesis   not synthesis

3) ____Fe_2O_3 (s) + ____SO_3 (g) → ____$Fe_2(SO_4)_3$ (s)

synthesis   not synthesis

4) ____NO (g) + ____O_2 (g) → ____NO_2 (g)

synthesis   not synthesis

5) ____$NaHCO_3$ (s) → ____Na_2CO_3 (s) + ____CO_2 (g) + ____H_2O (g)

synthesis   not synthesis

6) ____Br_2 (l) + ____MgI_2 (s) → ____$MgBr_2$ (s) + ____I_2 (s)

synthesis   not synthesis

Practice: Identifying Synthesis Reactions

...continued

7) _____ $FeBr_3$ (aq) + _____ $(NH_4)_2S$ (aq) → _____ Fe_2S_3 (aq) + _____ NH_4Br (aq)   synthesis   not synthesis

8) _____ Al (s) + _____ O_2 (g) → _____ Al_2O_3 (s)   synthesis   not synthesis

9) _____ NH_4NO_2 (s) → _____ N_2 (g) + _____ H_2O (l)   synthesis   not synthesis

10) _____ $C_4H_8O_2$ (l) + _____ O_2 (g) → _____ H_2O (g) + _____ CO_2 (g)   synthesis   not synthesis

11) _____ N_2 (g) + _____ O_2 (g) → _____ N_2O_5 (g)   synthesis   not synthesis

12) _____ Mn (s) + _____ CuCl (aq) → _____ Cu (s) + _____ $MnCl_2$ (s)   synthesis   not synthesis

Practice: Predicting Products of Synthesis Reactions

*Predict the **ionic products** of the synthesis reactions below. Balance them. Be sure to include physical states.*

1) _____Al (s) + _____O_2 (g) → _____ _____

2) _____CaO (s) + _____ H_2O (l) → _____ _____

3) _____Li_2O (s) + _____ H_2O (l) → _____ _____

4) _____K (s) + _____ Cl_2 (g) → _____ _____

5) _____Mg (s) + _____ O_2 (g) → _____ _____

6) _____SO_2 (g) + _____ H_2O (l) → _____ _____

Practice: Predicting Products of Synthesis Reactions

…continued

7) ____SO_3 (g) + ____ H_2O (l) → ____ _____

8) ____Al (s) + ____ Br_2 (l) → ____ _____

9) ____MgO (s) + ____ H_2O (l) → ____ _____

10) ____Na (s) + ____ P (s) → ____ _____

11) ____ Ca (s) + ____ O_2 (g) → ____ _____

12) ____ CO_2 (g) + ____ H_2O (l) → ____ _____

Self-Checking Practice: Synthesis Reactions

Determine whether the reactions below are synthesis reactions or another type of reaction. Highlight the correct answer and use the decoder below to place the corresponding letter in the row of boxes at the bottom of the page from 1 to 10. A message will appear!

#	Reaction	Synthesis reaction	Not a synthesis reaction
1	SO_3 (g) + H_2O (l) → H_2SO_4 (aq)	⊔	L
2	2 Al (s) + 3 $NiBr_2$ (aq) → 2 $AlBr_3$ (aq) + 3 Ni (s)	V	☐
3	A + B → AB	⊏	⊡
4	2 SO_2 (g) + O_2 (g) → 2 SO_3 (g)	☐	⊏
5	2 H_2O_2 (l) → 2 H_2O + O_2	⌐·	⌟
6	AB → A + B	⌐·	⌐·
7	C (s) + O_2 (g) → CO_2 (g)	··	Λ
8	AB + C → AC + B	>	☐
9	S (s) + O_2 (g) → SO_2 (g)	V	··
10	2 H_2 (l) + O_2 (g) → 2 H_2O (g)	V	⌐·

Decoder

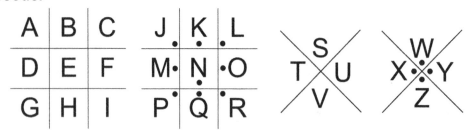

1	2	3	4	5	6	7	8	9	10

Decomposition Reactions

A **decomposition reaction** is a type of reaction where a compound breaks down into its elements or into two or more simpler compounds. These reactions often require heat or electricity.

The general form of this reaction is:

$$AB \rightarrow A + B$$

An example of a decomposition reaction is the breakdown of copper (II) carbonate into 2 smaller compounds:

$$CuCO_3\ (aq) \rightarrow CuO\ (s) + CO_2\ (g)$$

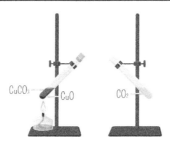

How can you identify a decomposition reaction?

- There is **1 reactant** and **2 or more products**.

How can you predict the products of a decomposition reaction?

- You will not *always* be able to predict the products of a decomposition reaction at this stage of your chemistry journey. Many reactions are complex and beyond the scope of high school.

- There are 4 main cases that you will encounter in this workbook:

> The elements produced are always going to be how they are found in nature. You need to determine their physical states and you need to remember your diatomic elements (HOFBrINCl)!

  1. A **compound** breaks down into its individual *elements*.
     - Ex: $2\ H_2O\ (l) \rightarrow 2\ H_2\ (g) + O_2\ (g)$

  2. A **metallic hydroxide** will break down into *water* and a *metal oxide*.
     - Ex: $Ca(OH)_2\ (s) \rightarrow H_2O\ (l) + CaO\ (s)$
       Metal oxides are solid

  3. A **metallic chlorate** will break down into *oxygen* and a *metal chloride*.
     - Ex: $Al(ClO_3)\ (s) \rightarrow O_2\ (g) + AlCl_3\ (s)$
       Metal chlorides are solid

  4. A **metallic carbonate** will break down into *carbon dioxide* and a *metal oxide*.
     - $CuCO_3\ (s) \rightarrow CO_2\ (g) + CuO\ (s)$

Practice: Identifying Decomposition Reactions

*Identify which of the following reactions are decomposition reactions by circling **decomp**. Balance them. (Note: You can balance the other reactions too if you need extra practice!*

1) ____Mg (s) + ____Cl$_2$ (g) → ____MgCl$_2$ (s)

decomp.   not decomp.

2) ____CH$_4$ (g) + ____O$_2$ (g) → ____H$_2$O (g) + ____CO$_2$ (g)

decomp.   not decomp.

3) ____NaCl (s) → ____Na (s) + ____Cl$_2$ (g)

decomp.   not decomp.

4) ____Al (s) + ____O$_2$ (g) → ____Al$_2$O$_3$ (s)

decomp.   not decomp.

5) ____KIO$_3$ (s) → ____KI (s) + ____O$_2$ (g)

decomp.   not decomp.

6) ____Sr(OH)$_2$ (aq) + ____HNO$_3$ (aq) → ____H$_2$O (l) + ____Sr(NO$_3$)$_2$ (aq)

decomp.   not decomp.

Practice: Identifying Decomposition Reactions

...continued

7) _____ Mg(H$_2$PO$_4$)$_2$ (aq) → _____Mg (s) + _____H$_2$ (g) + _____P (s) + _____O$_2$ (g)   decomp.   not decomp.

8) _____CaCO$_3$ (s) → _____CaO (s) + _____CO$_2$ (g)   decomp.   not decomp.

9) _____NI$_3$ (s) → _____N$_2$ (g) + _____I$_2$ (s)   decomp.   not decomp.

10) _____KClO$_3$ (s) + _____KCl (s) → _____O$_2$ (g)   decomp.   not decomp.

11) _____Al (s) + _____HCl (aq) → _____H$_2$ (g) + _____AlCl$_3$ (s)   decomp.   not decomp.

12) _____C (s) + _____O$_2$ (g) → _____CO$_2$ (g)   decomp.   not decomp.

 Struggling to balance equations like #10 or #11? If you end up with an odd number of oxygen or hydrogen on one side and an even number on the other side, use a decimal (x.5) in front of H$_2$ or O$_2$, and then double all of your coefficients to get whole numbers.

Practice: Predicting Products of Decomposition Reactions

Predict the products of the decomposition reactions below. Balance them. Be sure to include physical states.

<u>Part A</u>: *These compounds decompose into their **elements** with the addition of heat:*

1) ____$AlCl_3$ (s) → ____ _____ + ____ _____

2) ____Ag_2O (s) → ____ _____ + ____ _____

3) ____HgO (s) → ____ _____ + ____ _____

<u>Part B</u>: *The compounds below decompose according to the **rules on pg. 17**.*

4) ____Li_2CO_3 (s) → ____ _____ + ____ _____

5) ____$Ca(OH)_2$ (s) → ____ _____ + ____ _____

6) ____$Fe(OH)_2$ (s) → ____ _____ + ____ _____

P ractice: Predicting Products of Decomposition Reactions

…continued

7) ____$KClO_3$ (s) → ____ _____ + ____ _____

8) ____$MgCO_3$ (s) → ____ _____ + ____ _____

9) ____$Zn(OH)_2$ (s) → ____ _____ + ____ _____

Note: Remember that zinc always has a charge of +2

10) ____$Ni(ClO_3)_2$ (s) → ____ _____ + ____ _____

Note: Ni is multivalent, but use a charge of +2 here.

11) ____Na_2CO_3 (s) → ____ _____ + ____ _____

21

Self-Checking Practice: Decomposition Reactions

Take a look at the reactions below. Cross out the letter above each reaction that is NOT a decomposition reaction. The remaining letters need to be *unscrambled* to reveal the answer to the riddle.

I'm full of holes, yet I'm full of water. What am I?

O	R	A	J	P	C	T	E	K	B	L	I	G	Y	S	D	N
$BaCO_3\ (s) \rightarrow BaO\ (s) + CO_2\ (g)$	$H_2SO_4\ (aq) + Fe\ (s) \rightarrow H_2\ (g) + FeSO_4\ (aq)$	$Cl_2\ (g) + KBr \rightarrow KCl + Br_2\ (l)$	$2\ O_2\ (g) + H_2\ (g) \rightarrow 2\ H_2O\ (l)$	$2\ NaClO_3\ (s) \rightarrow 2\ NaCl\ (s) + 3\ O_2\ (g)$	$AB + CD \rightarrow AD + CB$	$Zn\ (s) + S\ (s) \rightarrow ZnS\ (s)$	$2\ H_2O\ (l) \rightarrow 2\ H_2\ (g) + O_2\ (g)$	$PbCl_2\ (aq) + AgNO_3\ (aq) \rightarrow Pb(NO_3)_2\ (aq) + AgCl\ (aq)$	$NH_3\ (g) + HCl\ (aq) \rightarrow NH_4Cl\ (aq)$	$AB + C \rightarrow CB + A$	$2\ C_4H_{10}\ (g) + 13\ O_2\ (g) \rightarrow 8\ CO_2\ (g) + 10\ H_2O\ (l)$	$2\ H_2O_2\ (aq) \rightarrow 2\ H_2O\ (l) + O_2\ (g)$	$HCl\ (aq) + NaOH\ (aq) \rightarrow NaCl\ (aq) + H_2O\ (l)$	$H_2CO_3\ (aq) \rightarrow H_2O\ (l) + CO_2\ (g)$	$C_2H_4\ (g) + 3\ O_2\ (g) \rightarrow 2\ CO_2\ (g) + 2\ H_2O\ (l)$	$AB \rightarrow A + B$

Answer: _____

Mixed Practice
Synthesis + Decomposition Reactions

*Classify each reaction as either **synthesis** or **decomposition***:

1) H_2 (g) + F_2 (g) → 2 HF (g) _____

2) CO_2 (g) + CaO (s) → $CaCO_3$ (s) _____

3) 4 Cr (s) + 3 O_2 (g) → 2 Cr_2O_3 (s) _____

4) 2 HCl (s) → H_2 (g) + Cl_2 (g) _____

5) 2 Rb_2O (s) → 2 Rb (s) + O_2 (g) _____

6) K (s) + O_2 (g) → K_2O (s) _____

7) $CaCO_3$ (s) → CaO (s) + CO_2 (g) _____

8) O_3 (g) → O (g) + O_2 (g) _____

9) 2 Na (s) + I_2 (s) → 2 NaI (s) _____

10) $ZnCO_3$ (s) → ZnO (s) + CO_2 (g) _____

11) $SrCl_2$ (s) → Sr (g) + Cl_2 (g) _____

12) 3 H_2 (g) + N_2 → 2 NH_3 (g) _____

Single Displacement Reactions

Single displacement reactions (also known as single replacement reactions) are chemical reactions where an element replaces another element in a compound. This type of reaction occurs when a *more reactive element* displaces a *less reactive element* from a compound.

The general form of this reaction is:

An example of a single displacement reaction is when solid iron displaces copper from a copper (II) sulfate solution to form solid copper and a solution of iron (II) sulfate:

$$Fe\ (s)\ +\ CuSO_4\ (aq)\ \rightarrow\ FeSO_4\ (aq)\ +\ Cu\ (s)$$

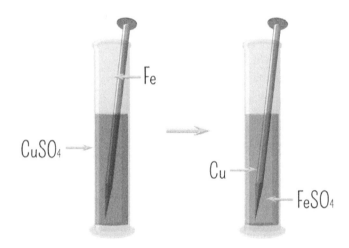

How can you identify a single displacement reaction?

- There is **1 element** reacting with **1 compound**, and the products are a **different element** and a **different compound**.

How can you predict the products of a single displacement reaction?

- Key idea: *The more reactive element will be part of the compound.*

- You will need to use a tool developed by scientists known as the **Activity Series** (see p. 25).

The Activity Series

The Activity Series (Metals)

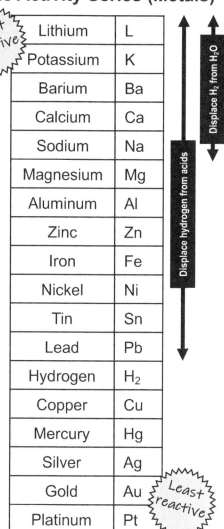

Lithium	L	
Potassium	K	
Barium	Ba	
Calcium	Ca	
Sodium	Na	
Magnesium	Mg	
Aluminum	Al	
Zinc	Zn	
Iron	Fe	
Nickel	Ni	
Tin	Sn	
Lead	Pb	
Hydrogen	H_2	
Copper	Cu	
Mercury	Hg	
Silver	Ag	
Gold	Au	
Platinum	Pt	

Most reactive

Least reactive

Displace H_2 from H_2O

Displace hydrogen from acids

The Activity Series (Halogens)

Most reactive

Fluorine	F_2
Chlorine	Cl_2
Bromine	Br_2
Iodine	I_2

Least reactive

How to Use The Activity Series:

- The *Activity Series* lists elements in terms of their reactivity, with the most reactive elements at the top of the list and the least reactive elements at the bottom.

- It is used to predict the products of a single displacement reaction.

- Look at the reactants of the reaction you're working with. If the lone element is a **metal**, you need to compare it with the **metal in the compound**.

   - The higher metal in the *Activity Series (Metals)* will be part of the <u>compound</u> in the products.

- If the lone element is a **halogen**, you need to compare it with the **halogen in the compound**.

   - The higher halogen in the *Activity Series (Halogens)* will be part of the <u>compound</u> in the products.

- Ex: Let's pretend we don't know the products of the reaction on p. 24: **Fe (s) + $CuSO_4$ (aq) → ???**

   - The element by itself is a metal, so we will use the *Activity Series (Metals)*.

   - Now, find both **Fe** and **Cu**. The metal that is closer to the top is going to form the compound with SO_4.

   - Since the more reactive metal (i.e. closer to the top) is **Fe**, it means that Fe will displace Cu from the compound and the products will be solid **Cu** and an **$FeSO_4$** solution.

Fe (s) + $CuSO_4$ (aq) → 2 Cu (s) + $FeSO_4$ (aq)

- *Note*: If solid Cu were placed in a solution of $FeSO_4$, no reaction would occur. Do you understand why?

Practice: Identifying
Single Displacement Reactions

*Identify which of the following reactions are single displacement reactions by circling **SD**. Balance them. (Note: You can balance the other reactions too if you need extra practice!)*

1) ____$FeBr_2$ (aq) + ____K_2CO_3 (aq) → ____$FeCO_3$ (s) + ____KBr (aq)   SD   not SD

2) ____Cu (s) + ____Ag_2SO_4 (aq) → ____$CuSO_4$ (aq) + ____Ag (s)   SD   not SD

3) ____Al (s) + ____$PbNO_3$ (aq) → ____Pb (s) + ____$Al(NO_3)_3$ (aq)   SD   not SD

4) ____Cl_2 (g) + ____MgI_2 (aq) → ____$MgCl_2$ (aq) + ____I_2 (s)   SD   not SD

5) ____CH_4 (g) + ____O_2 (g) → ____CO_2 (g) + ____H_2O (g)   SD   not SD

6) ____Na (s) + ____Cl_2 (g) → ____NaCl (s)   SD   not SD

Practice: Identifying
Single Displacement Reactions

...*continued*

7) ____Zn (s) + ____$CuSO_4$ (aq) → ____$ZnSO_4$ (aq) + Cu (s)

SD   not SD

8) ____HCl (aq) + ____NaOH (aq) → ____NaCl (aq) + ____H_2O (l)

SD   not SD

9) ____Zn (s) + ____HCl (aq) → ____$ZnCl_2$ (aq) + ____H_2 (g)

SD   not SD

10) ____V (s) + ____O_2 (g) → ____V_2O_5 (s)

SD   not SD

11) ____CsOH (aq) + ____H_3PO_4 (aq) → ____H_2O (l) + ____Cs_3PO_4 (aq)

SD   not SD

12) ____Na (s) + ____H_2O (l) → ____NaOH (aq) + ____H_2 (g)

SD   not SD

13) ____Rb_3AsO_4 (s) → ____Rb (s) + ____As (s) + ____O_2 (g)

SD   not SD

Practice: Predicting Products of Single Displacement Reactions

*Use the Activity Series to predict the **products** of the single displacement reactions below. Balance them. Be sure to include physical states. If no reaction occurs, write **<u>NO REACTION</u>**.*

1) _____Fe (s) + _____$CuSO_4$ (aq) → _____ _____ + _____ _____

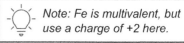

Note: Fe is multivalent, but use a charge of +2 here.

2) _____Ag (s) + _____HCl (aq) → _____ _____ + _____ _____

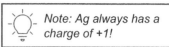

Note: Ag always has a charge of +1!

3) _____Pb (s) + _____$CuCl_2$ (aq) → _____ _____ + _____ _____

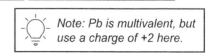

Note: Pb is multivalent, but use a charge of +2 here.

4) _____Al (s) + _____$ZnSO_4$ (aq) → _____ _____ + _____ _____

5) _____Cl_2 (g) + _____NaI (aq) → _____ _____ + _____ _____

6) _____Zn (s) + _____$Mg(NO_3)_2$ (l) → _____ _____ + _____ _____

Practice: Predicting Products of Single Displacement Reactions

…continued

7) ____Mg (s) + ____AgNO$_3$ (aq) → ____ _____ + ____ _____

8) ____Cu (s) + ____ H$_2$SO$_4$ (aq) → ____ _____ + ____ _____

9) ____I$_2$ (s) + ____SrCl$_2$ (aq) → ____ _____ + ____ _____

10) ____Ba (s) + ____H$_2$O (l) → ____ _____ + ____ _____

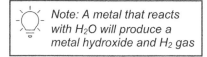 *Note: A metal that reacts with H$_2$O will produce a metal hydroxide and H$_2$ gas*

11) ____F$_2$ (g) + ____CaBr$_2$ (aq) → ____ _____ + ____ _____

12) ____Na (s) + ____CuSO$_4$ (aq) → ____ _____ + ____ _____

Self-Checking Practice:
Single Displacement Reactions

Use the Activity Series to determine if each reaction will occur. Highlight the correct answer and place the corresponding letters in the blank spaces at the bottom of the page from 1 to 14. A message will appear!

#	Reaction	Reaction occurs	No reaction occurs
4	Ni (s) + NaNO$_3$ (aq) → ???	RUT	SMA
11	Pb (s) + MgSO$_4$ (aq) → ???	LIN	KUR
8	Al (s) + CuCl$_2$ (aq) → ???	WO	TR
3	Mg (s) + PbSO$_4$ (aq) → ???	CEI	PLU
13	Cu (s) + AgNO$_3$ (aq) → ???	NEG	SHA
5	Ag (s) + KMnO$_4$ (aq) → ???	BE	GI
14	Au (s) + CaCl$_2$ (aq) → ???	YU	UT
1	Mg (s) + Zn(OH)$_2$ (aq) → ???	SCI	FRE
9	Zn (s) + FeBr$_2$ (aq) → ???	RK	LS
6	Na (s) + AlI$_3$ (aq) → ???	CT	TR
12	Ca (s) + K$_2$CO$_3$ (aq) → ???	MARI	TVON
10	I$_2$ (s) + AgCl (aq) → ???	E	S
2	Hg (s) + NaOH (aq) → ???	RI	EN
7	Sn (s) + H$_2$SO$_4$ (aq) → ???	HAT	CUD

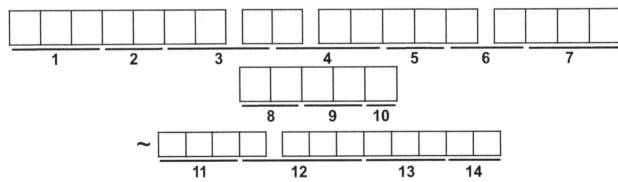

Mixed Practice
Synthesis, Decomposition, + Single Displacement Reactions

*Classify each reaction as **synthesis, decomposition**, or **single displacement**.*

1) C_2H_4 (g) + H_2O (g) → C_2H_5OH (l) _____

2) Pb (s) + $FeSO_4$ (aq) → Fe (s) + $PbSO_4$ (aq) _____

3) 2 Na (s) + Cl_2 (g) → 2 NaCl (s) _____

4) N_2 (g) + 3 H_2 (g) → 2 NH_3 (g) _____

5) 3 Pb (s) + 2 H_3PO_4 (aq) → 3 H_2 (g) + $Pb_3(PO_4)_2$ (aq) _____

6) 2 NH_4NO_3 (s) → N_2O (g) + H_2O (g) _____

7) $CaCO_3$ (s) → CaO (s) + CO_2 (g) _____

8) 2 NH_4NO_3 (s) → 2 N_2 (g) + O_2 (g) + 2 H_2O (g) _____

9) 2 K (s) + Cl_2 (g) → 2 KCl (s) _____

10) 2 Al (s) + 3 $CuSO_4$ (aq) → 3 Cu (s) + $Al_2(SO_4)_3$ (aq) _____

11) 2 Ag_2O (s) → 4 Ag (s) + O_2 (g) _____

12) F_2 (g) + 2 KI (aq) → 2 KF (aq) + I_2 (s) _____

Double Displacement Reactions

A **double displacement reactions** (also known as a double replacement reaction) is a chemical reaction where the positive ions (cations) and negative ions (anions) of two compounds switch places to form two new compounds. These occur in aqueous solutions.

The general form of this reaction is:

$$AB + CD \rightarrow AD + CB$$

An example of a double displacement reaction is when a copper (II) sulfate solution mixes with a solution of sodium hydroxide to form a solution of sodium sulfate and solid copper (II) hydroxide.

$$CuSO_4 \text{ (aq)} + 2\,NaOH \text{ (aq)} \rightarrow Na_2SO_4 \text{ (aq)} + Cu(OH)_2 \text{ (s)}$$

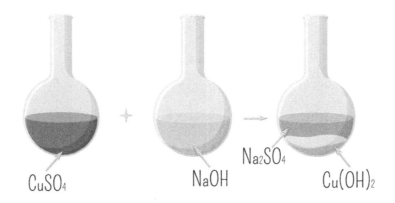

$CuSO_4$ $NaOH$ Na_2SO_4 $Cu(OH)_2$

How can you identify a double displacement reaction?

- There are **2 aqueous compounds** reacting, and the products are a **2 different compounds.**

- 1 of the products will no longer be aqueous (most often it will be solid, but it can also be water or a gas).

How can you predict the products of a double displacement reaction?

- Key idea: *Elements of 2 compounds will trade places, and one compound will have a change of state.*

- We will be focusing on double displacement reactions that form a *solid precipitate* in the products.

- You will need to use a tool developed by scientists known as the *Solubility Rules* (found on p. 33).

The Solubility Rules

How to Use The Solubility Rules:

- The *Solubility Rules* shows us whether combinations of ions will be **soluble** (i.e. aqueous solutions) or be **insoluble** (i.e. solid precipitates).

- Ex: Let's pretend we don't know the products of the reaction on p. 32:

$$CuSO_4 \text{ (aq)} + NaOH \text{ (aq)} \rightarrow \text{???}$$

  - We need to look at what new compounds will form in a DD reaction. Each **cation** will pair with a new **anion** (i.e. Cu^{2+} will bond with OH^- and Na^+ will bond with SO_4^{2-}).

  - We will consult the *Solubility Rules* to determine the physical states of these products.

    - Hydroxides are **insoluble**, and Cu^{2+} is <u>not</u> an exception. **$Cu(OH)_2$** is insoluble and will have an **(s)** symbol.

    - Sodium is an alkali metal, and all compounds containing alkali metals are soluble. **Na_2SO_4** is soluble and has an **(aq)** symbol.

> $CuSO_4 \text{ (aq)} + 2\,NaOH \text{ (aq)} \rightarrow Cu(OH)_2 \text{ (s)} + Na_2SO_4 \text{ (aq)}$

  - *Note*: If both potential products remain aqueous, we say that **NO REACTION** occurs.

Soluble Compounds	Exceptions
Alkali metal (Group IA) compounds (Li^+, Na^+, K^+, Cs^+, Rb^+)	None
Ammonium (NH_4^+) compounds	None
Nitrates (NO_3^-) Acetates (CH_3COO^-) Chlorates (ClO_3^-), Perchlorates (ClO_4^-)	None
Chlorides (Cl^-) Bromides (Br^-) Iodides (I^-)	Exceptions: Ag^+, Cu^+, Hg_2^{2+}, and Pb^{2+} compounds are insoluble.
Sulfates (SO_4^{2-})	Exception: Ag^+, Ba^{2+}, Ca^{2+}, Hg_2^{2+}, and Pb^{2+} compounds are insoluble.
Insoluble Compounds	**Exceptions**
Hydroxides (OH^-)	Exceptions: Alkali metal hydroxides, $Ba(OH)_2$, and $Ca(OH)_2$ are soluble.
Carbonates (CO_3^{2-}) Phosphates (PO_4^{3-})	Exceptions: Alkali metal and NH_4^+ compounds are soluble.
Sulfides (S^{2-})	Exceptions: Alkali metal, Alkaline Earth metal, and NH_4^+ compounds are soluble.

Practice: Identifying
Double Displacement Reactions

*Identify which of the following reactions are single displacement reactions by circling **DD**. Balance them. (Note: You can balance the other reactions too if you need extra practice!)*

1) ____AgClO$_3$ (aq) + ____K$_2$CO$_3$ (aq) → ____Ag$_2$CO$_3$ (s) + ____KClO$_3$ (aq)　　DD　　not DD

2) ____FeCl$_3$ (aq) + ____KOH (aq) → ____KCl (aq) + ____Fe(OH)$_3$ (s)　　DD　　not DD

3) ____C$_{22}$H$_{30}$O$_3$ (s) + ____O$_2$ (g) → ____CO$_2$ (g) + ____H$_2$O (g)　　DD　　not DD

4) ____Li (s) + ____O$_2$ (g) → ____Li$_2$O (s)　　DD　　not DD

5) ____AlF$_3$ (s) → ____Al (s) + ____F$_2$ (g)　　DD　　not DD

6) ____Li$_2$SO$_4$ (aq) + ____Ba(OH)$_2$ (aq) → ____BaSO$_4$ (s) + ____LiOH (aq)　　DD　　not DD

Practice: Identifying
Double Displacement Reactions

...continued

7) ____ C_5H_{12} (l) + ____ O_2 (g) → ____ H_2O (g) + ____ CO_2 (g)   *DD*   *not DD*

8) ____ $ZnSO_4$ (aq) + ____ $(NH_4)_2S$ (aq) → ____ ZnS (s) + ____ $(NH_4)_2SO_4$ (aq)   *DD*   *not DD*

9) ____ $CaCl_2$ (aq) + ____ Na_2CO_3 (aq) → ____ $NaCl$ (aq) + ____ $CaCO_3$ (s)   *DD*   *not DD*

10) ____ $AgNO_3$ (aq) + ____ Ni (s) → ____ $Ni(NO_3)_2$ (aq) + ____ Ag (s)   *DD*   *not DD*

11) ____ KI (aq) + ____ $Pb(NO_3)_2$ (aq) → ____ KNO_3 (aq) + ____ PbI_2 (s)   *DD*   *not DD*

12) ____ Na (s) → ____ H_2O (l) + ____ $NaOH$ (aq) + ____ H_2 (g)   *DD*   *not DD*

Practice: Predicting Products of Double Displacement Reactions

*Use the **Solubility Rules** to predict the **products** of the double displacement reactions below. Balance them (assume all multivalent ions use the same charge in the product formed). Be sure to include physical states. If no reaction occurs, write **NO REACTION**.*

1) ____$Ca(ClO_3)_2$ (aq) + ____$ZnSO_4$ (aq) → ____ _____ + ____ _____

2) ____$Ca(NO_3)_2$ (aq) + ____$CsCl$ (aq) → ____ _____ + ____ _____

3) ____$Ba(OH)_2$ (aq) + ____$Cu(NO_3)_2$ (aq) → ____ _____ + ____ _____

4) ____NH_4NO_3 (aq) + ____$CuCl_2$ (aq) → ____ _____ + ____ _____

5) ____$NaBr$ (aq) + ____$Pb(NO_3)_2$ (aq) → ____ _____ + ____ _____

6) ____K_3PO_4 (aq) + ____$CuCl_2$ (aq) → ____ _____ + ____ _____

Practice: Predicting Products of Double Displacement Reactions

…continued

7) ____NH₄Cl (aq) + ____AgNO₃ (aq) → ____ _____ + ____ _____

8) ____Li₂CO₃ (aq) + ____ NaNO₃ (aq) → ____ _____ + ____ _____

9) ____Na₂SO₄ (aq) + ____Ba(NO₃)₂ (aq) → ____ _____ + ____ _____

10) ____MgI₂ (aq) + ____AgClO₃ (aq) → ____ _____ + ____ _____

11) ____LiBr (aq) + ____CuCl₂ (aq) → ____ _____ + ____ _____

12) ____Cu(NO₃)₂ (aq) + ____NaI (aq) → ____ _____ + ____ _____

Self-Checking Practice:
Double Displacement Reactions

Use the **Solubility Rules** to determine the identity of the precipitate that will form when each pair of solutions is mixed. Find your answer on the next page and cross out the letter above it. The answer to the question will remain!

Copper (II) nitrate + ammonium hydroxide	Lead (II) chlorate + potassium iodide
Barium chloride + ammonium sulfate	Silver sulfate + sodium hydroxide
Tin (II) sulfate + potassium sulfide	Silver nitrate + lithium bromide
Lead (II) chlorate + cesium chloride	Magnesium iodide + ammonium carbonate
Lead (II) perchlorate + magnesium sulfate	Silver nitrate + calcium iodide
Aluminum nitrate + lithium phosphate	Magnesium perchlorate + sodium hydroxide
calcium nitrate + ammonium phosphate	Aluminum chlorate + sodium sulfide

Self-Checking Practice: Double Displacement Reactions

Do you like to hear chemistry jokes?

S	N	P	A	E	V	R	D	B	I	C	O	F
$PbSO_4$	$BaSO_4$	$NaClO_3$	$Mg(OH)_2$	Na_2SO_4	$AgBr$	NH_4NO_3	Al_2S_3	PbI_2	$KClO_3$	AgI	NH_4Cl	SnS

D	G	I	C	A	H	K	L	E	L	Y	D	R
K_2SO_4	$PbCl_2$	$Mg(ClO_4)_2$	NH_4I	$LiNO_3$	$Cu(OH)_2$	$AlPO_4$	$NaClO_4$	$MgCO_3$	$CsClO_3$	$Ca(NO_3)_2$	$Ca_3(PO_4)_2$	$AgOH$

Answer: _____

Mixed Practice
Synthesis, Decomposition, Single Displacement,
+ Double Displacement Reactions

*Classify each reaction as **synthesis, decomposition, single displacement,** or **double displacement.***

1) $2\,NaNO_3$ (s) $\rightarrow$ $2\,NaNO_2$ (s) + O_2 (g)   _____

2) $2\,CO$ (g) + O_2 (g) $\rightarrow$ $2\,CO_2$ (g)   _____

3) $2\,NaBr$ (aq) + Cl_2 (g) $\rightarrow$ $2\,NaCl$ (aq) + Br_2 (l)   _____

4) KBr (aq) + Li (s) $\rightarrow$ $LiBr$ (aq) + K (s)   _____

5) ABCD $\rightarrow$ AB + C + D   _____

6) $MgCl_2$ (aq) + Li_2CO_3 (aq) $\rightarrow$ $MgCO_3$ (s) + $2\,LiCl$ (aq)   _____

7) QR + ST $\rightarrow$ QT + SR   _____

8) $2\,Cs$ (s) + F_2 (g) $\rightarrow$ $2\,CsF$ (s)   _____

9) A + B + C $\rightarrow$ ABC   _____

10) Na_2S (aq) + $2\,HCl$ (aq) $\rightarrow$ $2\,NaCl$ (aq) + H_2S (g)   _____

11) XY + Z $\rightarrow$ XZ + Y   _____

12) $CuCO_3$ (s) $\rightarrow$ CuO (s) + CO_2 (g)   _____

Neutralization Reactions

A **neutralization reaction** is a chemical reactions that occurs between an acid and a base to produce a salt and water. It is a sub-type of double displacement reaction. It can be helpful to recognize these more specifically since acids and bases play an important role in our world.

The general form of this reaction is:

An example of a neutralization reaction is when hydrochloric acid and sodium hydroxide solution are mixed to produce a solution of sodium chloride and water:

$$HCl\ (aq)\ +\ NaOH\ (aq)\ \rightarrow\ NaCl\ (aq)\ +\ H_2O\ (l)$$

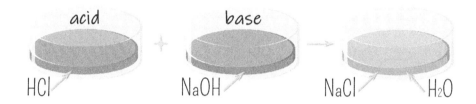

How can you identify a neutralization reaction?

- The reactants are an <u>**acid**</u> and a <u>**base**</u> and the products are an aqueous <u>**salt**</u> and <u>**water**</u>.
  - An **acid** is a substance that produces hydrogen ions (**H⁺**) in water (ex: HCl, H_2SO_4, HCO_3, HNO_3, etc.).
  - A **base*** is a substance that produces hydroxide ions (**OH⁻**) in water (ex: $LiOH$, $NaOH$, $Ca(OH)_2$, etc.).
  - Note: a **salt** is any ionic compound – not just sodium chloride! (This is a common misconception).

How can you predict the products of a neutralization reaction?

- <u>Key idea</u>: *Elements of 2 ionic compounds will trade places, and a new ionic compound (aka a salt) and water are formed.*

- This is the category of double displacement reactions that produce *water* as a product. The **hydrogen (H^+)** from the acid bonds with the **hydroxide (OH^-)** of the base to produce **H_2O**.

> *A base with hydroxide is considered a <u>strong base</u>. Weak bases also exist but the chemistry is a bit different. They are not included in this workbook.

Practice: Identifying Neutralization Reactions

*Identify which of the following reactions are neutralization reactions by circling **neut**. Balance them. (Note: You can balance the other reactions too if you need extra practice!)*

1) ____$Mg(ClO_3)_2$ (aq) + ____Na (s) → ____$NaClO_3$ (aq) + ____Mg (s)   *neut.   not neut.*

2) ____$NaOH$ (aq) + ____HCl (aq) → ____$NaCl$ (aq) + ____ H_2O (l)   *neut.   not neut.*

3) ____ C_8H_{18} (l) + ____ O_2 (g) → ____ CO_2 (g) + ____ H_2O (g)   *neut.   not neut.*

4) ____$Ba(OH)_2$ (aq) + ____H_2SO_4 (aq) → ____$BaSO_4$ (aq) + ____ H_2O (l)   *neut.   not neut.*

5) ____NH_4OH (aq) + ____ HF (aq) → ____NH_4F (aq) + ____H_2O (l)   *neut.   not neut.*

6) ____H_2O (l) + ____CaO (s) → ____$Ca(OH)_2$ (aq)   *neut.   not neut.*

Practice: Identifying
Neutralization Reactions

...continued

7) _____ Al (s) + _____ O$_2$ (g) → _____ Al$_2$O$_3$ (s)   *neut. not neut.*

8) _____ NH$_3$ (g) + _____ H$_2$SO$_4$ (aq) → _____ (NH$_4$)$_2$SO$_4$ (aq)   *neut. not neut.*

9) _____ HClO$_3$ (aq) + _____ RbOH (aq) → _____ RbClO$_3$ (aq) + _____ H$_2$O (l)   *neut. not neut.*

10) _____ Ag$^+$ (aq) + _____ Cl$^-$ (aq) → _____ AgCl (s)   *neut. not neut.*

11) _____ Pb (s) + _____ H$_3$PO$_4$ (aq) → _____ H$_2$ (g) + _____ Pb$_3$(PO$_4$)$_2$ (s)   *neut. not neut.*

12) _____ Ca(OH)$_2$ (aq) + _____ HI (aq) → _____ H$_2$O (l) + _____ CaI$_2$ (aq)   *neut. not neut.*

Practice: Predicting Products of Neutralization Reactions

*Predict the **products** of the neutralization reactions below. Balance them (assume all multivalent ions use the same charge in the product as they did as in the reactants). Be sure to include physical states.*

1) ____CsOH (aq) + ____H_2CO_3 (aq) → ____ _____ + ____ _____

2) ____HBr (aq) + ____$Ba(OH)_2$ (aq) → ____ _____ + ____ _____

3) ____$Al(OH)_3$ (aq) + ____HCl (aq) → ____ _____ + ____ _____

4) ____$Zn(OH)_2$ (aq) + ____HNO_3 (aq) → ____ _____ + ____ _____

5) ____$HBrO_3$ (aq) + ____LiOH (aq) → ____ _____ + ____ _____

6) ____HNO_3 (aq) + ____NaOH (aq) → ____ _____ + ____ _____

Practice: Predicting Products of Neutralization Reactions

...continued

7) ____NH$_4$OH (aq) + ____HF (aq) → ____ _____ + ____ _____

8) ____Ca(OH)$_2$ (aq) + ____ H$_2$CO$_3$ (aq) → ____ _____ + ____ _____

9) ____H$_3$PO$_4$ (aq) + ____RbOH (aq) → ____ _____ + ____ _____

10) ____HI (aq) + ____Al(OH)$_3$ (aq) → ____ _____ + ____ _____

11) ____H$_2$SO$_4$ (aq) + ____NaOH (aq) → ____ _____ + ____ _____

12) ____MgOH (aq) + ____H$_2$S (aq) → ____ _____ + ____ _____

Self-Checking Practice: Neutralization Reactions

Determine the name of the salt that will be formed when each acid and base on the left are combined. Use a ruler to draw a straight line that connects the dot by the reactants with the dot by the salt. The line will cross through a number and two letters. Put the letters in the matching numbered box at the bottom of the page. A message will be revealed!

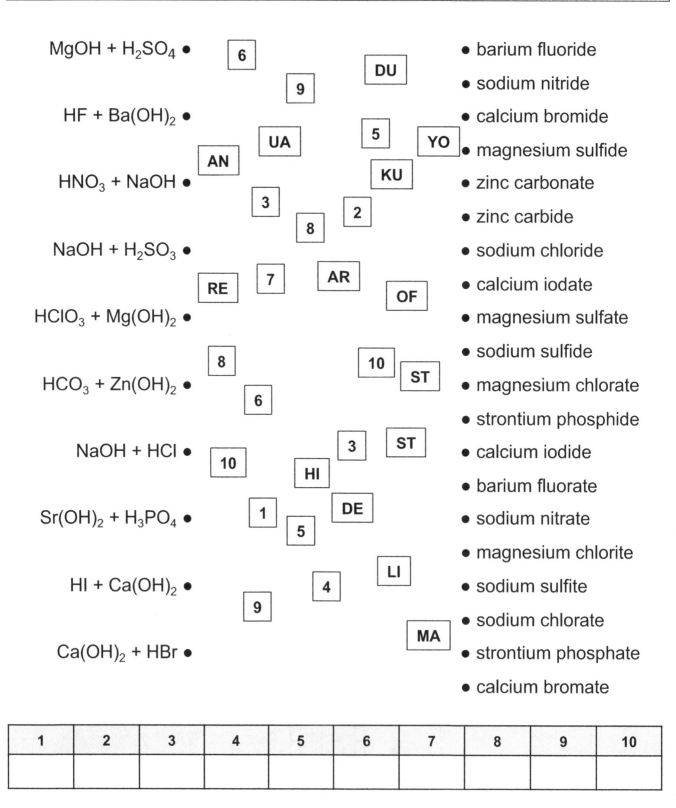

MgOH + H$_2$SO$_4$ •

HF + Ba(OH)$_2$ •

HNO$_3$ + NaOH •

NaOH + H$_2$SO$_3$ •

HClO$_3$ + Mg(OH)$_2$ •

HCO$_3$ + Zn(OH)$_2$ •

NaOH + HCl •

Sr(OH)$_2$ + H$_3$PO$_4$ •

HI + Ca(OH)$_2$ •

Ca(OH)$_2$ + HBr •

• barium fluoride
• sodium nitride
• calcium bromide
• magnesium sulfide
• zinc carbonate
• zinc carbide
• sodium chloride
• calcium iodate
• magnesium sulfate
• sodium sulfide
• magnesium chlorate
• strontium phosphide
• calcium iodide
• barium fluorate
• sodium nitrate
• magnesium chlorite
• sodium sulfite
• sodium chlorate
• strontium phosphate
• calcium bromate

1	2	3	4	5	6	7	8	9	10

Mixed Practice
Synthesis, Decomposition, Single Displacement, Double Displacement, + Neutralization Reactions

*Classify each reaction as **synthesis, decomposition, single displacement, double displacement,** or **neutralization.***

1) Li_2S (aq) + $MgBr_2$ (aq) → MgS (s) + 2 LiBr (aq) _____

2) NaCN (aq) + HBr (aq) → HCN (g) + NaBr (aq) _____

3) 2 $KClO_3$ (s) → 2 KCl (s) + 3 O_2 (g) _____

4) 2 K (s) + 2 H_2O (l) → 2 KOH (aq) + H_2 (g) _____

5) HX + YOH → XY + HOH _____

6) 2 $FeCl_3$ (aq) + 3 Zn (s) → 2 Fe (s) + 3 $ZnCl_2$ (aq) _____

7) Ca (s) + N_2 (g) → Ca_3N_2 (s) _____

8) HCl (aq) + KOH (aq) → H_2O (l) + KCl (aq) _____

9) 2 NaBr + $Ca(OH)_2$ → $CaBr_2$ + 2 NaOH _____

10) Na_2S (aq) + CaI_2 (aq) → 2 NaI (aq) + CaS (s) _____

11) SO_3 (g) + H_2O (l) → H_2SO_4 (aq) _____

12) 2 Na (s) + 2 H2O (l) → 2 NaOH (aq) + H_2 (g) _____

Combustion Reactions

A **combustion reaction** is a type of chemical reaction that involves hydrocarbons (i.e. compounds made of H, C, and sometimes O) that react with O_2. Heat and light are also released. These reactions have played a significant role in human history, providing warmth, light, and cooked food through the burning of various fuels like wood, fossil fuels, peat, or dung.

The general form of this reaction is:

$$C_xH_y + O_2 \rightarrow H_2O + CO_2$$

An example of a combustion reaction is when cellulose in wood burns in oxygen to produce water vapor and carbon dioxide gas.

$$C_6H_{10}O_5 \text{ (s)} + 6\, O_2 \text{ (g)} \rightarrow 5\, H_2O \text{ (g)} + 6\, CO_2 \text{ (g)}$$

CO₂
H₂O
O_2 is needed to keep the fire going
C_xH_y

How can you identify a combustion reaction?

- The reactants are a **hydrocarbon** (C_xH_y or $C_xH_yO_z$) and **O_2**, and the products are **CO_2** and **H_2O.**

How can you predict the products of a combustion reaction?

- Key idea: ***A fuel burns in oxygen, and carbon dioxide and water vapor are produced.***

There are actually 2 types* of combustion reactions: complete and incomplete.

1. **Complete Combustion:** The above example is complete combustion. When there is enough oxygen available, the products will be carbon dioxide and water vapor.

2. **Incomplete Combustion:** If there is insufficient oxygen available, some of the reactants may also be converted into C (soild carbon, aka soot) and carbon monoxide gas (CO). The general chemical equation would look like this:

$$C_xH_y \text{ (s)} + O_2 \text{ (g)} \rightarrow H_2O \text{ (g)} + CO_2 \text{ (g)} + C \text{ (s)} + CO \text{ (g)}$$

*This workbook will focus on complete combustion reactions

Balancing Combustion Reactions

Combustion reactions are often the trickiest to balance.

Since we always have C, H, and O is these reactions, we can ignore a lot of the MINOH acronym. It can be helpful to be more specific about our balancing strategy for combustion reactions.

Steps to Balancing Chemical Equations of Combustion Reactions:

1. Write out the **skeleton equation**.

2. Count the **number of atoms** of each type of element on either side of the arrow.

3. First, balance **carbon** atoms. Then, balance **hydrogen** atoms. Balance free **oxygen** last.

4. If you end up with an *odd number* of oxygens on one side and an *even number* of oxygens on the other side, use a decimal (*x.5*) in front of O_2, and then double all of your coefficients to get whole numbers.

Example 1: ___$C_6H_{10}O_5$ (s) + ___O_2 (g) → ___H_2O (g) + ___CO_2 (g)

(1) There are 6 carbons on the left and 1 on the right. Put a coefficient of 6 in front of CO_2.	___$C_6H_{10}O_5$ (s) + ___O_2 (g) → ___H_2O (g) + **6** CO_2 (g)
(2) There are 10 hydrogens on the left and 2 on the right. Put a coefficient of 5 in front of H_2O.	___$C_6H_{10}O_5$ (s) + ___O_2 (g) → **5** H_2O (g) + 6 CO_2 (g)
(3) There are 7 oxygens on the left and 17 on the right. Since 5 of the oxygens on the left are in the hydrocarbon, we can put a coefficient of 6 in front of O_2 in the equation.	$C_6H_{10}O_5$ (s) + **6** O_2 (g) → 5 H_2O (g) + 6 CO_2 (g)

Example 2: ___C_3H_8O (l) + ___O_2 (g) → ___H_2O (g) + ___CO_2 (g)

(1) There are 3 carbons on the left and 1 on the right. Put a coefficient of 3 in front of CO_2.	___C_3H_8O (l) + ___O_2 (g) → ___H_2O (g) + **3** CO_2 (g)
(2) There are 8 hydrogens on the left and 2 on the right. Put a coefficient of 4 in front of H_2O.	___C_3H_8O (l) + ___O_2 (g) → **4** H_2O (g) + 3 CO_2 (g)
(3) There are 3 oxygens on the left and 10 on the right. Since 1 of the oxygens on the left is in the hydrocarbon, we would need a coefficient of 4.5 in front of O_2 the equation.	___C_3H_8O (l) + **4.5** O_2 (g) → 4 H_2O (g) + 3 CO_2 (g)
(4) To get rid of the 4.5, we need to double all coefficients.	**2** C_3H_8O (l) + **9** O_2 (g) → **8** H_2O (g) + **6** CO_2 (g)

Practice: Identifying Combustion Reactions

*Identify which of the following reactions are combustion reactions by circling **combustion**.*
Balance them. (Note: You can balance the other reactions too if you need extra practice!

1) ____H_2SO_4 (aq) + ____NaOH (aq) → ____H_2O (l) + ____Na_2SO_4 (aq)   combustion   not combustion

2) ____CH_4 (g) + ____O_2 (g) → ____CO_2 (g) + ____H_2O (g)   combustion   not combustion

3) ____HF (aq) + ____LiOH (aq) → ____H_2O (l) + ____LiF (aq)   combustion   not combustion

4) ____P_4 (s) + ____Cl_2 (g) → ____PCl_5 (s)   combustion   not combustion

5) ____C_6H_{14} (g) + ____O_2 (g) → ____CO_2 (g) + ____H_2O (g)   combustion   not combustion

6) ____O_2 (g) + ____C_6H_6 (l) → ____H_2O (g) + ____CO_2 (g)   combustion   not combustion

Practice: Identifying Combustion Reactions

…continued

7) ____ C₂H₅OC₂H₅ (g) + ____O₂ (g) → ____H₂O (g) + ____CO₂ (g)   *combustion*   *not combustion*

8) ____C₂H₆ (g) + ____O₂ (g) → ____CO₂ (g) + ____ H₂O (g)   *combustion*   *not combustion*

9) ____NaCl (aq) + ____F₂ (g) → ____NaF (s) + Cl₂ (g)   *combustion*   *not combustion*

10) ____C₃H₈O (l) + ____O₂ (g) → ____H₂O (g) + ____CO₂ (g)   *combustion*   *not combustion*

11) ____C₂₅H₅₂ (s) + ____O₂ (g) → ____CO₂ (g) + ____ H₂O (g)   *combustion*   *not combustion*

12) ____CO₂ (g) + ____H₂O (l) → ____C₆H₁₂O₆ + ____O₂ (g)   *combustion*   *not combustion*

Practice: Predicting Products of Combustion Reactions

*Predict the **products** of the combustion reactions below. Balance them. Be sure to include physical states.*

1) ____C_3H_8 (g) + ____O_2 (g) → ____ _____ + ____ _____

2) ____C_9H_{20} (l) + ____O_2 (g) → ____ _____ + ____ _____

3) ____$C_{12}H_{22}O_{11}$ (s) + ____O_2 (g) → ____ _____ + ____ _____

4) ____C_4H_9OH (l) + ____O_2 (g) → ____ _____ + ____ _____

5) ____$C_{11}H_{24}$ (l) + ____O_2 (g) → ____ _____ + ____ _____

6) ____CH_3OH (l) + ____O_2 (g) → ____ _____ + ____ _____

Practice: Predicting Products of Combustion Reactions

…continued

7) ____C_5H_{10} (g) + ____O_2 (g) → ____ _____ + ____ _____

8) ____$C_{10}H_{22}$ (l) + ____ O_2 (g) → ____ _____ + ____ _____

9) ____C_7H_{16} (l) + ____O_2 (g) → ____ _____ + ____ _____

10) ____C_3H_8O (l) + ____O_2 (g) → ____ _____ + ____ _____

11) ____C_4H_{10} (g) + ____O_2 (g) → ____ _____ + ____ _____

12) ____C_2H_5OH (l) + ____O_2 (g) → ____ _____ + ____ _____

Self-Checking Practice: Combustion Reactions

Balance each combustion reaction. Then, use the coefficients in the boxes and the decoder to reveal the secret message.

▶ ☐ C_2H_2 (g) + ____O_2 (g) → ____H_2O (g) + ____CO_2 (g)

❖ ____C_4H_8 (g) + ☐ O_2 (g) → ____CO_2 (g) + ____ H_2O (g)

★ ____C_3H_7OH (g) + ☐ O_2 (g) → ____CO_2 (g) + ____ H_2O (g)

⌘ ____C_8H_{16} (l) + ☐ O_2 (g) → ____H_2O (g) + ____CO_2 (g)

♳ ____C_3H_8 (g) + ____O_2 (g) → ____ CO_2 (g) + ☐ H_2O (g)

Ω ____$C_{13}H_{28}$ (g) + ☐ O_2 (g) → ____CO_2 (g) + ____ H_2O (g)

⚑ ☐ $C_6H_{12}O_6$ (s) + ____O_2 (g) → ____CO_2 (g) + ____ H_2O (g)

◉ ____C_5H_{12} (g) + ____O_2 (g) → ☐ CO_2 (g) + ____ H_2O (g)

Decoder

1	2	3	4	5	6	7	8	9	10	11	12	13
E	N	C	R	L	U	P	K	F	V	Y	S	H

14	15	16	17	18	19	20	21	22	23	24	25	26
A	J	X	O	I	T	B	Z	Q	D	M	W	G

★	❖	⚑	◉	Ω	❖	♳	▶	⌘

Mixed Practice 1
Synthesis, Decomposition, Single Displacement,
Double Displacement, Neutralization Reactions, + Combustion

*Classify each reaction as **synthesis, decomposition, single displacement, double displacement, neutralization** or **combustion.***

1) $4 C_5H_9O + 27 O_2 \rightarrow 20 CO_2 (g) + 18 H_2O (g)$ _____

2) $PbCO_3 (aq) \rightarrow PbO (s) + CO_2 (g)$ _____

3) $Li_2S (aq) + 2 AgNO_3 (aq) \rightarrow 2 LiNO_3 (aq) + Ag_2S (s)$ _____

4) $P_2O_5 (g) + 3 H_2O (l) \rightarrow 2 H_3PO_4 (aq)$ _____

5) $C_3H_6O + 4 O_2 (g) \rightarrow 3 CO_2 (g) + 3 H_2O (g)$ _____

6) $2 NaOH (l) \rightarrow Na_2O (s) + H_2O (l)$ _____

7) $AlBr_3 (aq) + H_3PO_4 (aq) \rightarrow AlPO_4 (s) + 3 HBr (aq)$ _____

8) $HBr (aq) + NaOH (aq) \rightarrow H_2O (l) + NaBr (aq)$ _____

9) $H_3PO_4 (aq) + 3 LiOH (aq) \rightarrow 3 H_2O (l) + Li_3PO_4 (aq)$ _____

10) $2 Ti (s) + 2 Cl_2 \rightarrow 2 TiCl_3 (s)$ _____

11) $Fe (s) + 2 AgCH_3COO (aq) \rightarrow 2 Ag (s) + Fe(CH_3COO)_2 (aq)$ _____

12) $Cd (s) + I_2 (s) \rightarrow CdI_2 (s)$ _____

Mixed Practice 2
Synthesis, Decomposition, Single Displacement, Double Displacement, Neutralization, + Combustion Reactions

Convert each scenario into a balanced chemical equation that includes physical states. Classify it as one of the 6 reactions explored in this workbook.

1) Sulfuric acid and a solution of lithium hydroxide are mixed together to produce a salt and water.

   *Note: When a compound is described as a "solution" it means that it is **aqueous**.*

   Type of reaction: _____

2) A chunk of magnesium is placed in nitric acid. Bubbles form!

   *Note: Nitric acid has the chemical formula HNO_3. Remember that acids are always **aqueous**.*

   Type of reaction: _____

3) Carbon dioxide gas and water can be combined to form carbonic acid.

   Note: Carbonic acid has the chemical formula H_2CO_3.

   Type of reaction: _____

4) When heated, lithium carbonate will decompose to form a solid metal oxide and carbon dioxide gas. *Hint: What must the metal be?*

   Type of reaction: _____

Mixed Practice 3
Synthesis, Decomposition, Single Displacement, Double Displacement, Neutralization, + Combustion Reactions

…continued

5) A solution of silver nitrate is added to a solution of sodium chloride. A white precipitate forms (*Psst…the solubility rules on p.33 can help you identify the solid compound*).

> *Note: Remember that silver always has a charge of +1!*

Type of reaction: _____

6) Solid potassium metal is placed in a solution of magnesium bromide. A solution of potassium bromide is formed and a new metal begins to precipitate.

Type of reaction: _____

7) Liquid pentane (C_5H_{12}) burns in oxygen to form carbon dioxide and water vapor.

Type of reaction: _____

8) Ammonia gas (NH_3) and hydrogen chloride gas react to form ammonium chloride.

> *Remember that ionic compounds are always solid unless in a solution*

Type of reaction: _____

Mixed Practice 4
Synthesis, Decomposition, Single Displacement,
Double Displacement, Neutralization, + Combustion Reactions

…continued

9) Solutions of copper (II) nitrate and sodium hydroxide are mixed and a precipitate of copper (II) hydroxide is formed (along with a solution of sodium nitrate).

Type of reaction: _____

10) Isopropyl alcohol (C_3H_7OH) is burned in excess oxygen. Isopropyl alcohol is a common liquid used as a household disinfectant, antiseptic, and solvent.

> *Hint: What are the products when a hydrocarbon reacts with oxygen?*

Type of reaction: _____

11) Aqueous sodium hydroxide is added to aqueous hydrochloric acid. A pH strip is used to test the resulting solution and it shows that it has a neutral pH of 7.

Type of reaction: _____

12) Some molten (i.e. *liquid*) sodium chloride undergoes electrolysis to break it down into its elements.

Type of reaction: _____

SOLUTIONS

Solutions

Self-Checking Practice: Balanced or Unbalanced?
(p. 10)

Answer: Look up at the stars and not down at your feet

Practice: Identifying Synthesis Reactions
(p. 12)

1) $2 Na (s) + Cl_2 (g) \rightarrow 2 NaCl (s)$ **(synthesis)**
2) $2 NaOH (aq) + H_2SO_4 (aq) \rightarrow Na_2SO_4 (aq) + 2 H_2O$ **(not synthesis)**
3) $Fe_2O_3 (s) + 3 SO_3 (g) \rightarrow Fe_2(SO_4)_3 (s)$ **(synthesis)**
4) $2 NO (g) + O_2 (g) \rightarrow 2 NO_2 (g)$ **(synthesis)**
5) $2 NaHCO_3 (s) \rightarrow Na_2CO_3 (s) + CO_2 (g) + H_2O (g)$ **(not synthesis)**
6) $Br_2 (l) + MgI_2 (s) \rightarrow MgBr_2 (s) + I_2 (s)$ **(not synthesis)**
7) $2 FeBr_3 (aq) + 3 (NH_4)_2S (aq) \rightarrow Fe_2S_3 (aq) + 6 NH_4Br (aq)$ **(not synthesis)**
8) $4 Al (s) + 3 O_2 (g) \rightarrow 2 Al_2O_3 (s)$ **(synthesis)**
9) $NH_4NO_2 (s) \rightarrow N_2 (g) + 2 H_2O (l)$ **(not synthesis)**
10) $C_4H_8O_2 (l) + 5 O_2 (g) \rightarrow 4 H_2O (g) + 4 CO_2 (g)$ **(not synthesis)**
11) $2 N_2 (g) + 5 O_2 (g) \rightarrow 2 N_2O_5 (g)$ **(synthesis)**
12) $Mn (s) + 2 CuCl (aq) \rightarrow 2 Cu (s) + MnCl_2 (s)$ **(not synthesis)**

Practice: Predicting Products of Synthesis Reactions
(p. 14)

1) $4 Al (s) + 3 O_2 (g) \rightarrow 2 Al_2O_3 (s)$
2) $CaO (s) + H_2O (l) \rightarrow Ca(OH)_2 (aq)$
3) $Li_2O (s) + H_2O (l) \rightarrow 2 LiOH (aq)$
4) $2 K (s) + Cl_2 (g) \rightarrow 2 KCl (s)$
5) $2 Mg (s) + O_2 (g) \rightarrow 2 MgO (s)$
6) $SO_2 (g) + H_2O (l) \rightarrow H_2SO_3 (aq)$
7) $SO_3 (g) + H_2O (l) \rightarrow H_2SO_4 (aq)$
8) $2 Al (s) + 3 Br_2 (l) \rightarrow 2 AlBr_3 (s)$
9) $MgO (s) + H_2O (l) \rightarrow Mg(OH)_2 (aq)$
10) $3 Na (s) + P (s) \rightarrow Na_3P (s)$
11) $2 Ca (s) + O_2 (g) \rightarrow 2 CaO (s)$
12) $CO_2 (g) + H_2O (l) \rightarrow H_2CO_3 (aq)$

Self-Checking Practice:
Synthesis Reactions
(p. 16)

Answer: Be fearless

Solutions

...continued

Practice: Identifying Decomposition Reactions
(p. 18)

1) Mg (s) + Cl_2 (g) → $MgCl_2$ **(not decomp.)**
2) CH_4 (g) + 2 O_2 (g) → 2 H_2O (g) + CO_2 (g) **(not decomp.)**
3) 2 $NaCl$ (s) → 2 Na (s) + Cl_2 (g) **(decomp.)**
4) 4 Al (s) + 2 O_2 (g) → 2 Al_2O_3 (s) **(not decomp.)**
5) 2 KIO_3 (s) → 2 KI (s) + 3 O_2 (g) **(decomp.)**
6) $Sr(OH)_2$ (aq) + 2 HNO_3 (aq) → 2 H_2O (l) + $Sr(NO_3)_2$ (aq) **(not decomp.)**
7) $Mg(H_2PO_3)_2$ (aq) → Mg (s) + 2 H_2 (g) + 2 P (s) + 4 O_2 (g) **(decomp.)**
8) $CaCO_3$ (s) → CaO (s) + CO_2 (g) **(decomp.)**
9) 2 NI_3 (s) → N_2 (g) + 3 I_2 (s) **(decomp.)**
10) 2 $KClO_3$ (s) + 2 KCl (s) → 3 O_2 (g) **(not decomp.)**
11) 2 Al (s) + 6 HCl (aq) → 3 H_2 (g) + 2 $AlCl_3$ (s) **(not decomp.)**
12) C (s) + O_2 (g) → CO_2 (g) **(not decomp.)**

Practice: Predicting Products of Decomposition Reactions
(p. 20)

1) 2 $AlCl_3$ (s) → 2 Al (s) + 3 Cl_2 (g)
2) 2 Ag_2O (s) → 4 Ag (s) + O_2 (g)
3) 2 HgO (s) → 2 Hg (l) + O_2 (g)
4) Li_2CO_3 (s) → CO_2 (g) + Li_2O (s)
5) $Ca(OH)_2$ (s) → CaO (s) + H_2O (l)
6) $Fe(OH)_2$ (s) → FeO (s) + H_2O (l)
7) 2 $KClO_3$ (s) → 3 O_2 (g) + 2 KCl (s)
8) $MgCO_3$ (s) → CO_2 (g) + MgO (s)
9) $Zn(OH)_2$ (s) → ZnO (s) + H_2O (l)
10) $Ni(ClO_3)_2$ (s) → 3 O_2 (g) + $NiCl_2$ (s)
11) Na_2CO_3 (s) → CO_2 (g) + Na_2O (s)

Self-Checking Practice: Decomposition Reactions
(p. 22)

Answer: sponge

Mixed Practice: Synthesis + Decomposition Reactions
(p. 23)

1) Synthesis
2) Synthesis
3) Synthesis
4) Decomposition
5) Decomposition
6) Synthesis
7) Decomposition
8) Decomposition
9) Synthesis
10) Decomposition
11) Decomposition
12) Synthesis

Solutions

...continued

Practice: Identifying Single Displacement Reactions (p. 26)

1) $FeBr_2$ (aq) + K_2CO_3 (aq) → $FeCO_3$ (s) + 2 KBr (aq) **(not SD)**
2) Cu (s) + Ag_2SO_4 (aq) → $CuSO_4$ (aq) + 2 Ag (s) **(SD)**
3) Al (s) + 3 $PbNO_3$ (aq) → 3 Pb (s) + $Al(NO_3)_3$ (aq) **(not SD)**
4) Cl_2 (g) + MgI_2 (aq) → $MgCl_2$ + I_2 (s) **(SD)**
5) CH_4 (g) + 2 O_2 (g) → CO_2 (g) + 2 H_2O (g) **(not SD)**
6) 2 Na(s) + Cl_2 (g) → 2 NaCl (s) **(not SD)**
7) Zn (s) + $CuSO_4$ (aq) → $ZnSO_4$ (aq) + Cu (s) **(SD)**
8) HCl (aq) + NaOH (aq) → NaCl (aq) + H_2O (l) **(not SD)**
9) Zn (s) + 2 HCl (aq) → $ZnCl_2$ (aq) + H_2 (g) **(SD)**
10) 4 V (s) + 5 O_2 (g) → 2 V_2O_5 (s) **(not SD)**
11) 3 CsOH (aq) + H_2PO_4 (aq) → 3 H_2O (l) + Cs_3PO_4 (aq) **(not SD)**
12) 2 Na (s) + 2 H_2O (l) → 2 NaOH (aq) + H_2 (g) **(SD)**
13) Rb_3AsO_4 (s) → 3 Rb (s) + As (s) + 2 O_2 (g) **(not SD)**

Practice: Predicting Products of Single Displacement Reactions (p. 28)

1) Fe (s) + $CuSO_4$ (aq) → $FeSO_4$ (aq) + Cu (s)
2) Ag (s) + HCl (aq) → NR
3) Pb (s) + $CuCl_2$ (aq) → $PbCl_2$ (aq) + Cu (s)
4) 2 Al (s) + 3 $ZnSO_4$ (aq) → $Al_2(SO_4)_3$ (aq) + 3 Zn (s)
5) Cl_2 (g) + 2 NaI (aq) → 2 NaCl (aq) + 2 I_2 (s)
6) Zn (s) + $Mg(NO_3)_2$ (aq) → NR
7) Mg (s) + 2 $AgNO_3$ (aq) → $Mg(NO_3)_2$ (aq) + 2 Ag (s)
8) Cu (s) + H_2SO_4 (aq) → NR
9) I_2 (s) + $SrCl_2$ (aq) → NR
10) Ba (s) + 2 H_2O (l) → $Ba(OH)_2$ (aq) + H_2 (g)
11) F_2 (g) + $CaBr_2$ (aq) → CaF_2 (aq) + Br_2 (l)
12) 2 Na (s) + $CuSO_4$ (aq) → Na_2SO_4 (aq) + Cu (s)

Self-Checking Practice: Single Displacement Reactions (p. 30)

Answer: Science is magic that works. ~Kurt Vonnegut

Mixed Practice: Synthesis, Decomposition, + Single Displacement Reactions (p. 31)

1) Synthesis
2) Single displacement
3) Synthesis
4) Synthesis
5) Single displacement
6) Decomposition
7) Decomposition
8) Decomposition
9) Synthesis
10) Single displacement
11) Decomposition
12) Single displacement

Solutions

...*continued*

Practice: Identifying Double Displacement Reactions
(p. 34)

1) $2\ AgClO_3\ (aq) + K_2CO_3\ (aq) \rightarrow Ag_2CO_3\ (s) + 2\ KClO_3\ (aq)$ **(DD)**
2) $FeCl3\ (aq) + 3\ OH\ (aq) \rightarrow 3\ KCl\ (aq) + Fe(OH)3\ (s)$ **(DD)**
3) $C_{22}H_{30}O_3\ (s) + 28\ O_2\ (g) \rightarrow 22\ CO_2\ (g) + 15\ H_2O\ (g)$ **(not DD)**
4) $4\ Li\ (s) + O_2\ (g) \rightarrow 2\ Li_2O\ (s)$ **(not DD)**
5) $2\ AlF_3\ (s) \rightarrow 2\ Al\ (s) + 3\ F_2\ (g)$ **(not DD)**
6) $Li_2SO_4\ (aq) + Ba(OH)_2\ (aq) \rightarrow BaSO_4\ (s) + 2\ LiOH\ (aq)$ **(DD)**
7) $C_5H_{12}\ (l) + 8\ O_2\ (g) \rightarrow 6\ H_2O\ (g) + 5\ CO_2\ (g)$ **(not DD)**
8) $ZnSO_4\ (aq) + (NH_4)_2S\ (aq) \rightarrow ZnS\ (s) + (NH_4)_2SO_4\ (aq)$ **(DD)**
9) $CaCl_2\ (aq) + Na_2CO_3\ (aq) \rightarrow 2\ NaCl\ (aq) + CaCO_3\ (s)$ **(DD)**
10) $2\ AgNO_3\ (aq) + Ni\ (s) \rightarrow Ni(NO_3)_2\ (aq) + 2\ Ag\ (s)$ **(not DD)**
11) $2\ KI\ (aq) + Pb(NO_3)_2\ (aq) \rightarrow 2\ KNO_3\ (aq) + PbI_2\ (s)$ **(DD)**
12) $2\ Na\ (s) \rightarrow 2\ H_2O\ (l) + 2\ NaOH\ (aq) + H_2\ (g)$ **(DD)**

Practice: Predicting Products of Double Displacement Reactions
(p. 36)

1) $Ca(ClO_3)_2\ (aq) + ZnSO_4\ (aq) \rightarrow CaSO_4\ (s) \rightarrow Zn(ClO_3)_2\ (aq)$
2) $Ca(NO_3)_2\ (aq) + CsCl \rightarrow$ NO REACTION
3) $Ba(OH)_2\ (aq) + Cu(NO_3)_2\ (aq) \rightarrow Cu(OH)_2\ (s) + Ba(NO_3)_2\ (aq)$
4) $NH_4NO_3\ (aq) + CuCl_2\ (aq) \rightarrow$ NO REACTION
5) $2\ NaBr\ (aq) + Pb(NO_3)_2\ (aq) \rightarrow PbBr_2\ (s) + 2\ NaNO_3\ (aq)$
6) $2\ K_3PO_4\ (aq) + 3\ CuCl_2\ (aq) \rightarrow Cu_3(PO_4)_2\ (s) + 6\ KCl\ (aq)$
7) $NH_4Cl\ (aq) + AgNO_3\ (aq) \rightarrow NH_4NO_3\ (aq) + AgCl\ (s)$
8) $Li_2CO_3\ (aq) + NaNO_3\ (aq) \rightarrow$ NO REACTION
9) $Na_2SO_4\ (aq) + Ba(NO_3)_2\ (aq) \rightarrow BaSO_4\ (s) + 2\ NaNO_3\ (aq)$
10) $MgI_2\ (aq) + 2\ AgClO_3\ (aq) \rightarrow Mg(ClO_3)_2\ (aq) + 2\ AgI\ (s)$
11) $2\ LiBr\ (aq) + CuCl_2\ (aq) \rightarrow 2\ LiCl\ (aq) + CuBr_2\ (s)$
12) $Cu(NO_3)_2\ (aq) + 2\ NaI\ (aq) \rightarrow 2\ NaNO_3\ (aq) + CuI_2\ (s)$

Self-Checking Practice: Double Displacement Reactions
(p. 39)

Answer: Periodically

Mixed Practice: Synthesis, Decomposition, Single Displacement,
+ Double Displacement Reactions
(p. 40)

1) Decomposition
2) Synthesis
3) Single displacement
4) Single displacement
5) Decomposition
6) Double displacement
7) Double displacement
8) Synthesis
9) Synthesis
10) Double displacement
11) Single displacement
12) Decomposition

Solutions

...continued

Practice: Identifying Neutralization Reactions
(p. 42)

1) $Mg(ClO_3)_2$ (aq) + 2 Na (s) → $NaClO_3$ (aq) + Mg (s) **(not neut.)**
2) NaOH (aq) + HCl (aq) → NaCl (aq) + H_2O (l) **(neut.)**
3) 2 C_8H_{18} (l) + 25 O_2 (g) → 16 CO_2 (g) + 18 H_2O (g) **(not neut.)**
4) $Ba(OH)_2$ (aq) + H_2SO_4 (aq) → $BaSO_4$ (aq) + 2 H_2O (l) **(neut.)**
5) NH_4OH (aq) + HF (aq) → NH_4F (aq) + H_2O (l) **(neut.)**
6) H_2O (l) + CaO (s) → $Ca(OH)_2$ (aq) **(not neut.)**
7) 4 Al (s) + 3 O_2 (g) → 2 Al_2O_3 (s) **(not neut.)**
8) 2 NH_3 (g) + H_2SO_4 (aq) → $(NH_4)_2SO_4$ (aq) **(not neut.)**
9) $HClO_3$ (aq) + RbOH (aq) → $RbClO_3$ (aq) + H_2O (l) **(neut.)**
10) Ag^+ (aq) + Cl^- (aq) → AgCl (s) **(not neut.)**
11) 3 Pb (s) + 2 H_3PO_4 (aq) → 3 H_2 (g) + $Pb_3(PO_4)_2$ (s) **(not neut.)**
12) $Ca(OH)_2$ (aq) + 2 HI (aq) → 2 H_2O (l) + CaI_2 (aq) **(neut.)**

Practice: Predicting Products of Neutralization Reactions
(p. 44)

1) 2 CsOH (aq) + H_2CO_3 (aq) → Cs_2CO_3 (aq) + 2 H_2O (l)
2) 2 HBr (aq) + $Ba(OH)_2$ (aq) → $BaBr_2$ (aq) + 2 H_2O (l)
3) $Al(OH)_3$ (aq) + 3 HCl (aq) → $AlCl_3$ (aq) + 3 H_2O (l)
4) $Zn(OH)_2$ (aq) + 2 HNO_3 (aq) → $Zn(NO_3)_2$ (aq) + 2 H_2O (l)
5) $HBrO_3$ (aq) + LiOH (aq) → $LiBrO_3$ (aq) + H_2O (l)
6) HNO_3 (aq) + NaOH (aq) → $NaNO_3$ (aq) + H_2O (l)
7) NH_4OH (aq) + HF (aq) → NH_4F (aq) + H_2O (l)
8) $Ca(OH)_2$ (aq) + H_2CO_3 (aq) → $CaCO_3$ (aq) + 2 H_2O (l)
9) H_3PO_4 (aq) + 3 RbOH (aq) → Rb_3PO_4 (aq) + 3 H_2O (l)
10) HI (aq) + $Al(OH)_3$ (aq) → AlI_3 (aq) + H_2O (l)
11) H_2SO_4 (aq) + NaOH (aq) → Na_2SO_4 (aq) + H_2O (l)
12) MgOH (aq) + H_2S (aq) → MgS (aq) + H_2O (l)

Self-Checking Practice: Neutralization Reactions
(p. 46)

Answer: You are made of stardust

Mixed Practice: Synthesis, Decomposition, Single Displacement,
Double Displacement, + Neutralization Reactions
(p. 47)

1) Double displacement
2) Double displacement
3) Decomposition
4) Single displacement
5) Neutralization
6) Single displacement
7) Synthesis
8) Neutralization
9) Double displacement
10) Double displacement
11) Synthesis
12) Double displacement

Solutions

...*continued*

Practice: Identifying Combustion Reactions
(p. 50)

1) H_2SO_4 (aq) + 2 NaOH (aq) → 2 H_2O (l) + Na_2SO_4 (aq) **(not combustion)**
2) CH_4 (g) + 2 O_2 (g) → CO_2 (g) + 2 H_2O (g) **(combustion)**
3) HF (aq) + LiOH (aq) → H_2O (l) + LiF (aq) **(not combustion)**
4) P_4 (s) + 10 Cl_2 (g) → 4 PCl_5 (s) **(not combustion)**
5) 2 C_6H_{14} (g) + 19 O_2 (g) → 12 CO_2 (g) + 14 H_2O (g) **(combustion)**
6) 15 O_2 (g) + 2 C_6H_6 (l) → 6 H_2O (g) + 12 CO_2 (g) **(combustion)**
7) $C_2H_5OC_2H_5$ (g) + 6 O_2 (g) → 5 H_2O (g) + 4 CO_2 (g) **(combustion)**
8) 2 C_2H_6 (g) + 7 O_2 (g) → 4 CO_2 (g) + 6 H_2O (g) **(combustion)**
9) 2 NaCl (aq) + F_2 (g) → 2 NaF (s) + Cl_2 (g) **(not combustion)**
10) 2 C_3H_8O (l) + 9 O_2 (g) → 8 H_2O (g) + 6 CO_2 (g) **(combustion)**
11) $C_{25}H_{52}$ (s) + 38 O_2 (g) → 25 CO_2 (g) + 26 H_2O (g) **(combustion)**
12) 6 CO_2 (g) + 6 H_2O (l) → $C_6H_{12}O_6$ (s) + 6 O_2 (g) **(not combustion)**

Practice: Predicting Products of Combustion Reactions
(p. 52)

1) C_3H_8 (g) + 5 O_2 (g) → 3 CO_2 (g) + 4 H_2O (g)
2) C_9H_{20} (l) + 14 O_2 (g) → 9 CO_2 (g) + 10 H_2O (g)
3) $C_{12}H_{22}O_{11}$ (s) + 12 O_2 (g) → 12 CO_2 (g) + 11 H_2O (g)
4) C_4H_9OH (l) + 6 O_2 (g) → 4 CO_2 (g) + 5 H_2O (g)
5) $C_{11}H_{24}$ (l) + 17 O_2 (g) → 11 CO_2 (g) + 12 H_2O (g)
6) 2 CH_3OH (l) + 3 O_2 (g) → 2 CO_2 (g) + 4 H_2O (g)
7) 2 C_5H_{10} (g) + 15 O_2 (g) → 10 CO_2 (g) + 10 H_2O (g)
8) 2 $C_{10}H_{22}$ (l) + 31 O_2 (g) → 20 CO_2 (g) + 22 H_2O (g)
9) C_7H_{16} (l) + 11 O_2 (g) → 7 CO_2 (g) + 8 H_2O (g)
10) 2 C_3H_8O (l) + 9 O_2 (g) → 6 CO_2 (g) + 8 H_2O (g)
11) 2 C_4H_{10} (g) + 13 O_2 (g) → 8 CO_2 (g) + 10 H_2O (g)
12) C_2H_5OH (l) + 4 O_2 (g) → 2 CO_2 (g) + 3 H_2O (g)

Self-Checking Practice: Combustion Reactions
(p. 54)

Answer: Fuel burns

Mixed Practice 1: Synthesis, Decomposition, Single Displacement, Double Displacement, Neutralization, + Combustion Reactions
(p. 55)

1) Combustion
2) Decomposition
3) Double displacement
4) Synthesis
5) Combustion
6) Decomposition
7) Double displacement
8) Neutralization
9) Neutralization
10) Synthesis
11) Single displacement
12) Synthesis

Solutions

...continued

Mixed Practice 2: Synthesis, Decomposition, Single Displacement, Double Displacement, Neutralization, + Combustion Reactions (p. 56)

1) H_2SO_4 (aq) + 2 LiOH (aq) → 2 H_2O (l) + Li_2SO_4 (aq) **(neutralization)**
2) Mg (s) + 2 HNO_3 (aq) → $Mg(NO_3)_2$ (aq) + H_2 **(single displacement)**
3) CO_2 (g) + H_2O (l) → H_2CO_3 (aq) **(synthesis)**
4) Li_2CO_3 (s) → CO_2 (g) + Li_2O (s) **(decomposition)**

Mixed Practice 3: Synthesis, Decomposition, Single Displacement, Double Displacement, Neutralization, + Combustion Reactions (p. 57)

5) $AgNO_3$ (aq) + NaCl (aq) → AgCl (s) + $NaNO_3$ (aq) **(double displacement)**
6) 2 K (s) + $MgBr_2$ (aq) → 2 KBr (aq) + Mg (s) **(single displacement)**
7) C_5H_{12} (l) + 8 O_2 (g) → 5 CO_2 (g) + 6 H_2O **(combustion)**
8) NH_3 (g) + HCl (g) → NH_4Cl (s) **(synthesis)**

Mixed Practice 3: Synthesis, Decomposition, Single Displacement, Double Displacement, Neutralization, + Combustion Reactions (p. 58)

9) $Cu(NO_3)_2$ (aq) + 2 NaOH (aq) → $Cu(OH)_2$ (s) + 2 $NaNO_3$ (aq) **(double displacement)**
10) 2 C_3H_7OH (l) + 9 O_2 (g) → 6 CO_2 (g) + 8 H_2O (g) **(combustion)**
11) NaOH (aq) + HCl (aq) → NaCl (aq) + H_2O (l) **(neutralization)**
12) 2 NaCl (l) → 2 Na (s) + Cl_2 (g) **(decomposition)**

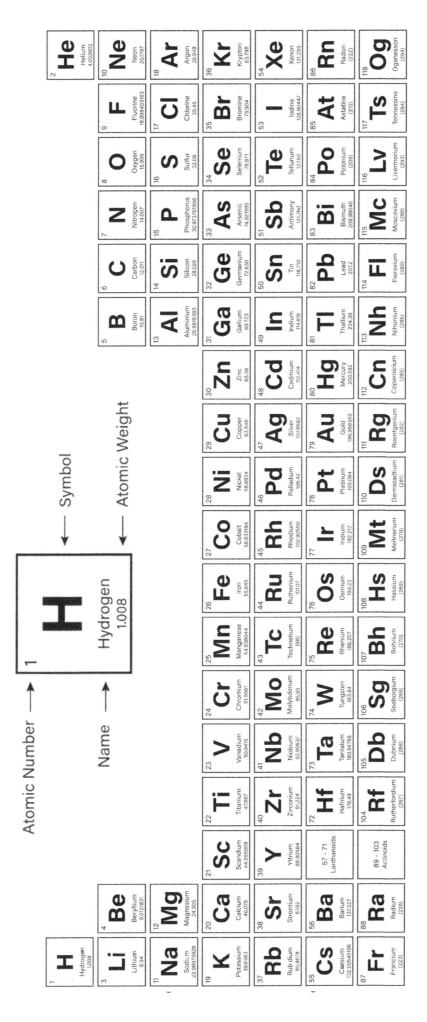

Reference Tables

Common Multivalent Metals

Metal	Element Symbol	Ion Symbols	Ion names
Cobalt	Co	Co^{2+} Co^{3+}	Cobalt (II) Cobalt (III)
Chromium	Cr	Cr^{2+} Cr^{3+}	Chromium (II) Chromium (III)
Copper	Cu	Cu^+ Cu^{2+}	Copper(I) Copper(II)
Iron	Fe	Fe^{2+} Fe^{3+}	Iron (II) Iron (III)
Lead	Pb	Pb^{2+} Pb^{4+}	Lead (II) Lead (IV)
Manganese	Mn	Mn^{2+} Mn^{4+}	Manganese (II) Manganese (IV)
Mercury	Hg	Hg^+ Hg^{2+}	Mercury (I) Mercury (II)
Tin	Sn	Sn^{2+} Sn^{4+}	Tin (II) Tin (IV)
Titanium	Ti	Ti^{3+} Ti^{4+}	Titanium (III) Titanium (IV)
Vanadium	V	V^{3+} V^{5+}	Vanadium (III) Vanadium (V)

Common Polyatomic Ions

Name	Ion	Name	Ion
Acetate	$C_2H_3O^-$	Hydroxide	OH^-
Ammonium	NH_4^+	Hypochlorite	ClO^-
Bicarbonate	HCO_3^-	Nitrate	NO_3^-
Bromate	BrO_3^-	Nitrite	NO_2^-
Carbonate	CO_3^{2-}	Perchlorate	ClO_4^-
Chlorate	ClO_3^-	Permanganate	MnO_4^-
Chlorite	ClO_2^-	Phosphate	PO_4^{3-}
Chromate	CrO_4^{2-}	Phosphite	PO_3^{3-}
Cyanide	CN^-	Sulfate	SO_4^{2-}
Dichromate	$Cr_2O_7^{2-}$	Sulfite	SO_3^{2-}

Reference Tables

Common Acids	
Name	**Chemical Formula**
Acetic acid	$HC_2H_3O_2$
Bromic acid	$HBrO_3$
Carbonic acid	H_2CO_3
Chlorous acid	$HClO_2$
Hydrobromic acid	HBr
Hydrochloric acid	HCl
Hydrocyanic acid	HCN
Hydrofluoric acid	HF
Hydroiodic acid	HI
Hydrosulfuric acid	H_2S
Hypobromous acid	$HBrO$
Hypochlorous acid	$HClO$
Hypoiodous acid	HIO
Iodic acid	HIO_3
Nitric acid	HNO_3
Nitrous acid	HNO_2
Perbromic acid	$HBrO_4$
Perchloric acid	$HClO_4$
Periodic acid	HIO_4
Phosphoric acid	H_3PO_4
Sulfuric acid	H_2SO_4
Sulfurous acid	H_2SO_3

Reference Tables

The Activity Series (Metals)

Lithium	L
Potassium	K
Barium	Ba
Calcium	Ca
Sodium	Na
Magnesium	Mg
Aluminum	Al
Zinc	Zn
Iron	Fe
Nickel	Ni
Tin	Sn
Lead	Pb
Hydrogen	H_2
Copper	Cu
Mercury	Hg
Silver	Ag
Gold	Au
Platinum	Pt

Displace H_2 from H_2O

Displace hydrogen from acids

The Activity Series (Halogens)

Fluorine	F_2
Chlorine	Cl_2
Bromine	Br_2
Iodine	I_2

Reference Tables

The Solubility Rules

Soluble Compounds	Exceptions
Alkali metal (Group IA) compounds (Li^+, Na^+, K^+, Cs^+, Rb^+)	None
Ammonium (NH_4^+) compounds	None
Nitrates (NO_3^-) Acetates (CH_3COO^-) Chlorates (ClO_3^-), Perchlorates (ClO_4^-)	None
Chlorides (Cl^-) Bromides (Br^-) Iodides (I^-)	Exceptions: Ag^+, Cu^+, Hg_2^{2+}, and Pb^{2+} compounds are insoluble.
Sulfates (SO_4^{2-})	Exception: Ag^+, Ba^{2+}, Ca^{2+}, Hg_2^{2+}, and Pb^{2+} compounds are insoluble.
Insoluble Compounds	**Exceptions**
Hydroxides (OH^-)	Exceptions: Alkali metal hydroxides, $Ba(OH)_2$, and $Ca(OH)_2$ are soluble.
Carbonates (CO_3^{2-}) Phosphates (PO_4^{3-})	Exceptions: Alkali metal and NH_4^+ compounds are soluble.
Sulfides (S^{2-})	Exceptions: Alkali metal, Alkaline Earth metal, and NH_4^+ compounds are soluble.

Want a **FREE** resource to help you master chemical reactions?

Made in the USA
Las Vegas, NV
07 May 2024